To
Pauline Chase Harvey.
May the stars of wonder embrace you

ABOVE RUBIES
Women of the Bible

Blow away the dust
of ages and let your heart
seek old mysteries

Guanetta Gordon

Drawing by Pat Scher

GUANETTA GORDON

Above Rubies

Women of the Bible

Proverbs 31:10

Who can find a virtuous woman?
for her price is far above rubies

THE GOLDEN QUILL PRESS
Publishers
Francestown   New Hampshire

Library of Congress Catalog Card Number 76-19716

ISBN 0-8233-0250-4

Printed in the United States of America

Acknowledgments to the following for their assistance, advice, and inspiration: Shirley Jones, Jeanne Thompson, Gene Clark, Eileen Sandford, William Turner, Pat Scher, and Lynell Gordon with thanks and appreciation.

CONTENTS

WOMEN OF THE NEW TESTAMENT

INTRODUCTION

The Bible holds first place on the best-seller list. It is a standard of great literature and historical fact with a mystical and spiritual revelation which the Holy Spirit blends together.

In studying each woman of the Bible I have tried to step in her shoes, turn back the centuries to her time and place, and experience as an actress, her life and problems.

Scripture usually gives only a skeleton story of what took place. Generally there is mention of an event in more than one book of the Bible. Other discoveries were gleaned from such books as the following: *Bible Dictionary*, by William Smith Lld.; *The Bible as History*, by Werner Keller; *The Old Testament Speaks*, by Samuel J. Schultz; *The Jewish Wars* and *Antiquities*, by Jewish Historian, Flavius Josephus, who lived 37-100 A.D.; *The Family Bible Encyclopedia*; and various other sources. One *National Geographic Magazine* of 1970 confirmed information which I had searched for, for many years. These, and a continuous study of the Bible are the sources I used.

I have changed no fact of Scripture, though I have dramatized what might have happened, surrounding the facts with researched information and interpretation, and by putting events together to conclude a story.

The concept of *Above Rubies* was conceived ten years ago. Through meditation and guidance the various women came alive to me in their own time. I found great pleasure in knowing these women. I often wondered what I might have done under such circumstances. The writing has been a great experience.

GUANETTA GORDON

DUST SHALL BE THE SERPENT'S MEAT

Genesis 3:2-4
Genesis 4:8-15

DUST SHALL BE THE SERPENT'S MEAT

Eve thought of crumbled Eden, wondered
if still the garden thrived beyond her view
of this strange desert. Guilt lay burning
as vitrol in her breast. She must subdue
her grief . . . for the gift was gone forever.
Here her roots must ever probe the deep
of earth to ease her constant thirsting
as restless winds of night held her from sleep
to remember the Cherubims that flourished
a flaming sword to seal off everything,
and send them forth in shame as outcasts,
to barren lands where they suffered the scorpion's
    sting.

Here her first born had slain his brother,
here the ground had tasted blood. Poor Cain
must henceforth wear the mark of evil,
a wanderer planting seed of sin and pain.
Eve looked on her infant, her consolation,
upon young Seth all future hope was placed.
"I think, you may find the way back to Eden
where all things perfect, were by a touch, engraced.
If God should grant it, think not too harshly
on your mother. Remember that she was very
    young
and foolish . . . one bowing of head to listen
to subtle flattery oozing from Satan's tongue."

13

STRANGE PARAGENESIS

Genesis 19:1, 12-26

The catastrophic destruction of Sodom and Gomorrah took place probably about 1900 B.C. Historic findings lead to the conclusion that these cities lay in an area now submerged beneath the southern section of the Dead Sea. Their destruction came about, it seems, through an earthquake and the explosion of natural gases.

A Phoenician priest used these words in his *Ancient History*, which has now been rediscovered: "The Vale of Sidimus (Sidim or Sodom) sank and became a lake, always evaporating."

Even today this area with its shining salt hills is desolate and anything near the Salt Sea in this locality is soon covered with a salt crust. Lot's wife when she tarried may have been suffocated by poisonous fumes.

The word *Paragenesis* — the formation of minerals in close contact, with a resulting interlocking of their crystals, as in granite, marble, etc. (in this case, salt).

STRANGE PARAGENESIS

For days the ominous threat tormented her mind,
that Sodom, city of splendor, had long remained
under judgment of God; must turn from wickedness.
The local rulers devised this image, entwined
with prophetic warning, to keep their subjects chained,
subservient, bowing before their aggressiveness
of tyranny, subjects to sing in a cage,
as birds that peck at sweetmeats, unmindful of cloud,
of wind, of hawk. To her, the wife of Lot,
each day was an opening blossom. She tried to gauge
the truth of rumor. Here, she felt endowed
with position, even wealth. Why believe this plot
of destruction, prepare herself to tear up roots
of permanence? Here, her children had grown secure
and she had guided them well from evil's trend.
Why should she listen to Lot's queer substitutes
for reason. Could even Abraham know, be sure
he had heard God's voice? In respect she would not
    offend
this relative who had often befriended them.
Last month he sent them a message, "Be prepared;
ask not for what, but face the dawn of tomorrow . . .
and tomorrow, with faith. Our God does not condemn
the righteous amid the lost." Through dusk she stared
at the skyline of Sodom, aware of some vague sorrow.
A black-veined moth fluttered to her shoulder, fell
to earth a lifeless omen . . . or was it chance?
Apprehension filled her heart, as it did that night
when Lot arose as one beneath a spell . . .

17

perhaps of doom, and left the house to glance
at funnel-clouds that cast a weird green light.
She was even more intense when he returned
with two strange men, or were they messengers, sent
as predicted? Yet would they come without disguise
with only a radiance, a lighted countenance that burned
with conviction? What quality gave their environment
the stamp of judgment? Was it the flame in their eyes?
As Lot washed their feet with trembling hands, she spread
the table, ordered slaves to prepare a feast.
Then the men spoke. "The Lord, thy God, doth despise
this city. If thou hath sons and daughters, wed,
with homes here, tell them leave before light has creased
the sky, and look not back where Sodom lies."
Then Lot hastened out while she moved as if held in
    trance,
how could she tell their daughters now asleep,
they too must leave. How could they bid farewell
to every treasure, be turned from home; vagrants
with only endless skies and hills to reap
as harvest? Blindly she packed their food. The smell
of the saltmarsh had blown far inland, dried her throat . . .
the acrid winds that blew against her cheek
were oppressive, squeezing her heart. She almost
    swooned . . .
A touch aroused her. The two strange men seemed
    remote
as they led them outside the city, where all was bleak,
and bade them go, as earth cracked in a jagged wound.

They ran in frantic confusion; she somehow moaned,
"Where, Lot, will we find the other children, where?"

18

"Do not look back for they did not believe . . .
I tried, and they but scoffed. Our God they disowned."

She paused and fell behind in the smoke thick air.
Perhaps they still might follow. She could not conceive
a life without them. Her very heartstrings were tied
about the pillars of old foundations; her soul
was not prepared, nor had she the strength, nor will
for this sudden evacuation; perhaps she could hide
and later return to find her loved ones. What toll
would death have claimed? She seemed ensnared in a still
white fog. She thought, I must look toward the future,
    blot
out the past. Yet she turned, tear blind. Perhaps they
    might run
to her, as so often they had done before.
Transfixed, she saw the earth split in fiery hot
abyss, flicking red-forked tongues; weird paragon
that lighted the great salt columns near the shore . . .
of the Dead Sea . . . where crysalite stones stood as ghosts.
She noticed a fallen bird in sodium shield,
a caked woolly sheep, a lizard, saline veiled.
She heard Lot call from the hill above the coast,
she tried to answer. The pungent fumes had sealed
her lips, she felt numb, her flesh was drawn and scaled.
In terror she struggled against the appalling dream,
release me, Lot, else soon I have enhaled
too much of this lethal vapor, this deadly steam . . .
here, Lot, here . . . she tried so hard to scream . . .

19

THE HEART WITHDRAWS

Genesis 21:9-10

THE HEART WITHDRAWS

A red lipped dawn enticed the sun across
the valley stirring now beneath the flame,
as Sarah listened to the rustling oaks
that grew in Hebron's mountains. Henna shrubs
had rooted near the spring and fragrance spread
from clustered heads of white to fill her tent,
so rolled to catch the breeze. She looked across
to hills that sealed off desert heat . . . today
the tribe of Abraham would celebrate
the birthday of their son, a festival
for Isaac, now a lad of two. A cock
began to crow and servants rose to start
their tasks. She too should rise but how she loved
these early hours to think on heart-tied dreams
and thank Jehovah for the blessed gift
of Isaac after all her barren years.
No longer could the handmaid Hagar scorn
the wife of Abraham as one accursed.
Now Sarah's gaze was drawn toward Hagar's tent,
for Ishmael, her sixteen year old son,
came dashing forth, a strange wild prince, who
    loathed
his young half brother, heir to Hebron lands.
He stood there, proud as some dark spirit, poised
for vengeance. Soon he called a group of lads
to gather round him . . . heaven knew for what!
Uneasiness swept Sarah's heart . . . for long
she'd tried to win young Ishmael. Twelve years
she taught him at her knee and loved his quick
responsive mind, yet never was he hers,

for Hagar saw to that, defying law
that gave the babe to mistress of the house
who owned the mother. Worst of all, she knew
that Hagar disobeyed and worshiped gods
of Pharoah, pagan idols which she kept
well hidden. Ishmael had learned the creeds
of Amon . . . not so strict as Abraham's
Jehovah. Sarah had become afraid
for Isaac's safety even though he held
Jehovah's blessing. Had not Cain struck down
his brother Abel? Had the parents watched,
perhaps the tragic act might not have been.
When serpent clouds began to form, the wise
took refuge . . . storm was swelling in the heart
of Ishmael. Soon now the boy must leave.
Let him and Hagar both be sent back home
to Egypt. Sarah knew she would be blamed
for sending them away, and folk would think
her jealous of the younger handmaid, still
she knew within her heart that Ishmael
with wild Egyptian blood relied on fate
instead of God, for blood was thicker, much,
than water. Let the tempest come, she must
reach tall to touch the stars within the soul.

THE DRIVEN LEAF

Genesis 21:11-21

THE DRIVEN LEAF

Her name was Hagar. Proud Egyptian blood
her heritage, though concubine she was
of Abraham. He once had held her near
his heart, admired her amber skin as smooth
as myrtle leaves, his lips had touched her hair . . .
remembrance still was sweet that fate had stamped
all honor on her name in bringing forth
an only son, named Ishmael, but stars
had turned facetious . . . after fourteen years
they favored Sarah who had given birth
to Isaac. Then the woman changed. With scorn
of hatred, aging Sarah used her wiles
in goading Abraham to banish both
the handmaid and her son. She said they mocked
the celebration given Isaac, now
that he was weaned at two years old. She claimed
they laughed with jealousy, with disrespect,
yet Hagar knew, by right, a man's first born
receives the blessing and inheritance . . .
but since she was a common lily, one
the wind had tossed aside, she bowed before
the wife and took all consequence. She looked
with loathing at her adversary, held
with pride her head, for Hagar still was young
and still desirable. Old Sarah must
not know that Hagar claimed no kinfolk now,
nor place to go. Poor Abraham still cared
for her and did not want to cast them out
though promises to Sarah did not change
the bitter gall that burned her withered breasts

27

as Abraham set Hagar free, and tried
to make them wait until a caravan
should pass through Hebron, wishing they depart
with escort back to Egypt. Hagar bowed
before her lord, refused to stay where they
were so unwanted. Ishmael's firm hand
took hold the burro's halter. Arm in arm
the son and mother started southward toward
the wilderness of Beersheba. As yet
the sun still lingered hot, and sand burned deep
their ankles. "Do not falter, Ishmael,
walk straight . . . do not look back. Pretend that we
are not afraid, for Sarah watches us."
A fan-foot lizard scurried for a rock
beside a clump of wild star thistles. Wind
coiled round their bodies, whipped the flesh as one
lone leaf from distant tamarisk blew past.
A flock of linnets winged toward water, back
from whence they came. The son and mother trudged
until a ridge of sand dunes hid them well.

Now Hagar slumpt, her wild dark eyes were wet,
"I am afraid my Ishmael. Perhaps
we should turn back, beg mercy. I know not
if we can walk this distance all alone."
She felt his rough young hand in hers. He smiled
encouragement and said, "We must go on
to Egypt. There I wish to live among
our own, and as a dove we'll find the way."
Now Hagar brightened. "I am only tired.
There is a place to rest by yonder mound . . .
to sleep beneath the stars. Tomorrow starts

another day, another life. Faint hearts,
as moon moths, flutter through a single night,
while birds can sing all night and fly at dawn."

CHAIN OF PROPHECY

Genesis 25:23-34
Genesis 27:1-46
Genesis 28:1-10

Rebekah has often been condemned for her part in deceiving her husband and winning the family inheritance for her favorite son, Jacob. The penalty she paid for her deed was that both sons were estranged from her and that she never saw either of them again in her lifetime. Yet, Rebekah remembered what God had revealed to her:

Genesis 25:23 "And the Lord said unto her, two nations are in thy womb, and two manner of people shall be separated from thy bowels; and the one people shall be stronger than the other people; and the elder shall serve the younger."

When the twins were born (*Genesis 25:25-26*) "The first came out red all over like an hairy garment and they called his name Esau. And after that came his brother out, and his hand took hold on Esau's heel; and his name was called Jacob."

When the boys were grown, Rebekah learned that her husband, Isaac, was ready to bestow the inheritance on Esau. Remembering God's choice she believed her husband was going against the will of God and intervened.

CHAIN OF PROPHECY

Rebekah stood on the walled roof garden, scanned
the hills and saw two horsemen riding in,
almost obscure in clouds of whirling sand,

and yet she knew her sons and how each twin
must vie in games to keep his self respect
though Esau mostly was the one to win.

It now appeared that Isaac would select
red Esau heir, and give his parental seal
of blessing . . . yet God had told her His elect.

Her sons held destined lives, the first to kneel
as servant. Esau had already sold
his right as eldest son for Jacob's meal,

but Isaac's heart was set. She must take hold
of Jacob, change the scheme of things. Goat's wool
on arms would feel like hair, and manifold

before weak eyes, a semblance of Esau. The full
impact of consequence was awesome when blame
was hers to bear, the sin indelible.

She would appeal to God to cleanse her name,
erase her guilt as smoke from altar flame.

Aftermath
The shadows on the wall had lengthened; dawn
was still an hour away, though sleep would not
return. Rebekah sighed, the paragon

33

of life was strange. If she could only blot
the past away . . . her part in changing fate.
Both sons in anger had turned against her plot,

for Esau, feeling cheated, burned with hate
and threatened his brother's life, while Jacob felt
his acquired inheritance a shameful weight.

Both sons had gone away. The first had dealt
a blow that pierced her heart though she explained . . .
For many moons she longed for Jacob, who dwelt

among her brother's people, and there had gained
two wives, while Esau in revenge had wed
with Canaanites, rejoiced that this had pained

his parents. Even Isaac, with scorn, had said
how wrong she was to act for God, and had deemed
her false. Regret changed nothing . . . shadows spread . . .

The angel death embraced . . . Rebekah dreamed
that Jacob kissed her lips . . . or so it seemed.

POMEGRANATES BUD FORTH

Genesis 29:16-28

The twelve tribes of Israel stemmed from the twelve sons of Jacob, each tribe being named after a chieftain son.

Leah was the unwanted and unloved wife of Jacob yet she became the mother of six sons. Her handmaiden Zilpah, bore two sons, and since it was Jewish law that children by a handmaiden became the property of the wife, Leah claimed eight of the sons of Jacob.

It must have been difficult for Leah to know that her husband loved her young sister, Rachel, and cared little for her except to perpetuate his family heritage. Yet through her, Jacob acquired great recognition, power, and prestige.

POMEGRANATES BUD FORTH

Leah watched the lovers
strolling hand in hand
beneath the olives.
Resentment, a liquid fire
that quavered as a volcano,
she held in check. This night
her husband, Jacob, would take
a second wife, his true love.
Since first he had set eyes
on Rachel, beautiful
as dawn and dusk combined
with moods to fascinate,
his desire was drawn to the flame.
Only Leah knew her sister
was in love with love itself,
and enjoyed all male attention;
while she, the homely one
with eyes so weak that sight
was held to narrow span,
yet could see the two embrace
was supposed to wish them joy.
Her brow was creased in frown,
her eyes drawn to red lined slits,
but the beauty that lived within
her heart and mind was real,
and there love rooted deep.

In spite of circumstances,
Leah felt deep gratitude
to her scheming father. He

had arranged the plan to wed
her to cousin Jacob, to fulfil
her consuming love for him.

The law was clear that an elder
daughter must be taken
before the others. Leah
would always cherish dreams
of her wedding night . . .
of Jacob's tenderness,
while stars circled round the moon,
with love, as night flowers, unfolding.
Jacob slept and pulled her close
within his arms, though her heart
had trembled as dawn erased
the dark, when Jacob's image
of Rachel changed to reality.
Even then he spared her pride
and touched her hair with kindness,
had spoken of its sheen.
When tears spilled from her eyes
he comforted her. "You were
a lovely bride, though both
of us were pawns of Laban
and him I seek to question."

Ah well, dear Jacob had honored
her position when Laban refused
to annul the bond while he bargained . . .
if Jacob promised to work
another seven years
then Rachel might also be his.

Leah knew that every wife
must be prepared to bow
to other wives, though Rachel
was such a gloating bride
and kept Jacob near her side
with yearning lips and within
clear view of the forsaken wife
who burned with jealousy.

She turned away. Perhaps
in time, if fate be kind,
she would present a strong son
to Jacob. Days when Rachel displayed
her fiery temperament,
she, Leah, would be waiting
to give her lord just due.
Perhaps in time she might
become the favored wife,
for beauty fades before
the vibrant glow of love.

THE SHADOW OF MANY MOONS

Genesis 31:11-20
Genesis 35:16-19

Rachel, enroute to Hebron, died in childbirth and was buried on the way to Ephrath, which is Bethlehem. She called this son Benoni, which meant "son of sorrow," but his father called him Benjamin.

Jacob set a pillar upon her grave: that is the pillar of Rachel's grave unto this day.

THE SHADOW OF MANY MOONS

The caravan was almost ready
and Rachel checked her list of items . . .
how strange it felt to leave
the only home she had ever known,
yet God had directed her husband Jacob
to return unto the land of Hebron,
to go while her father, Laban,
would be away six weeks
to survey the boundaries of his land.

Now excitement, the magic stone
of adventure, glittered in her mind.
Outside, the cattle drivers grumbled
that the herds were restless and ready to drive.
Rachel stepped to the door
to see her sister, Leah,
followed by her daughter, Dinah,
and eight tall sons, all dressed
for desert travel, striding forth
to mount their camels. Six sons
had Leah given Jacob, plus two
born of her handmaiden, Zilpah.

Envy swelled as a festering cloud
since she, Rachel, the most beloved wife
had one son, Joseph, flesh of her flesh,
her other two of handmaiden, Billah,
though always Leah's eight compared
to Rachel's three was a poisonous thorn.
Now Leah, the first wife, would hold

the honored place in the caravan
and at the journey's end would take
precedence with Jacob's family . . .
hot winds of bitterness dried her dreams.

To her father it mattered not
that he had cheated her
of the coveted title, "first wife"
but chose to saddle Jacob
with Leah by placing her
in the bridal chamber meant for Rachel.
He knew that after many toasts
of wine at the marriage feast, the groom
would never know his bride was not
the one of choice, till daybreak.
Then when Jacob confronted him
he shrewdly pointed out that Rachel
had been blessed at birth
with attributes of subtle charm
while Leah, the eldest must always
walk in her younger sister's shadow.
Still if Jacob wouid contract
to labor another seven years
he would be fair and give him
both of them, his dearest treasures.

Laban, being Laban,
had then demanded more and more
of Jacob's share of everything
and conveniently forgot to settle
an inheritance upon his daughters . . .
though Leah had created

her own value in sons,
while she, Rachel, ever
appeared a blighted flower . . .
until one day she bargained with Leah
and pledged that Jacob would be with her
that night in exchange for the precious Mandrakes
found by Reuben, Leah's son.
All barren women dreamed
of one day finding that illusive
plant with the two forked root
which no man could cultivate.
Thus it was that soon she expected
her first child, Joseph, now
a goodly son of eight.

Dawn was signaling departure
and a slave was beckoning her to come.
Leah and her many sons
were being hoisted to their mount.
She tightened the veil about her hair
and started out. Then justice
like the rising sun,
pierced her vengeful heart.
She turned back and went forthwith
into her father's private temple.
His household images . . .
set with precious gems
would balance his injustice.
By right he owed her these
for all her years of second place.
Possession of these special gods
would place her Jacob in position

to claim by law their inheritance
which now was due his wives.

Quickly she wrapped the gods in linen
and thought, when the camel is made to kneel
for me to mount, I will distract
the attention of the slave and hide
the images inside the camel furniture,
and no one need to know.
The gods themselves would deem me right,
perhaps might grant me another son
before the caravan reaches Hebron.

In jubilance she raced outside
and saw Jacob hurrying down the way
to see if anything was wrong.
She waved to him. He smiled
then signaled the caravan to move . . .
and what a train it was!
Jacob who had come to Haran
with nothing but clothes upon his back,
was returning in pride, for his yield
would equal all his own inheritance
that had waited all these years.

When the caravan reached
the little hill of poplars,
Rachel turned, looked back at the place
she would never see again . . .
she smiled without remorse.

BONE OF MY BONE

Exodus 2:1-10

According to Flavius Josephus, the Jewish Historian, the name of Pharaoh's daughter was Thermuthis.

BONE OF MY BONE

The wind sobbed through the bulrush flats and pierced
the heart of Jochebed, as callused hands
secured the last detail of one small ark.
She smoothed the lining, fingered it with love
before she laid her infant son inside.
He lay there waving small fat arms. Fear gripped
her soul as every heartbeat prayed that God
might strengthen her to carry out this plan
that verged on madness, trusting some divine
resource to intervene and save her child.
Once more she snatched him back to hold him close,
yet time was running out, for yesterday
a soldier caught a glimpse of him who cried,
and soon an agent would investigate
the child's background, for Jewish sons must die
beneath the sword, to balance Pharaoh's scale
of equal population. If the babe
should live she must relinquish every claim
to him, this pulse of heart, this flesh and bone.
Wet eyed she called her daughter, "Listen well,
my Miriam, let not the ark drift far
from shore nor catch among the reeds. Fear not,
the water is not deep along the bank,
but wait until Thermuthis comes to bathe,
then aim it true to reach the cove. Take care
that no one sees your presence. Let this child
be wrapped in mystery. The Princess wants
a child, I'm told. Perhaps she might appeal
to Pharaoh for his life. My little son,
I place you now beneath Jehovah's wings,

my heart is wrung with agony as hands
set you adrift. Go Miriam, take care,
while I return to work in Egypt's fields,
as tears collect in bottles which are stored
in vaults beneath divine protective seal.
My lips shall pray unless I faint . . . unless
I die . . . "

AS SPARKS FLY UPWARD

Exodus 2:21
Exodus 4:20-25
Exodus 18:1-6, 27

AS SPARKS FLY UPWARD

Zipporah's voice was well controlled to hide
frustration. I would speak with you my lord,
to plead once more for your benevolence.

How can you put aside our thirty years
of marriage, loving, sharing, being one?
Should all of life be changed because you claim
to sight a burning bush upon a hill
and are convinced you heard the voice of God?
Please hear me out my husband; in this land
there is a plant whose blossoms hold small cups
of oil, so volatile that when the sun
becomes too hot the bush bursts into flame.
Yes I recall, this one was burned yet not
consumed, a mystery indeed. Perhaps
you saw the crimson mistletoe in bloom,
its brilliant color would appear as fire.

I have been patient; even came with you
to Egypt, listened while you told your plan
to Aaron. True I can not fathom all
strange happenings to Pharoah's land while naught
befell the Israelites, but now you lead
your people far away . . . though Midian
has offered them a refuge. Moses, why
must you insist on lands to make your own
except for power to rule? Ah yes, I know
Jehovah, the invisible, divines
the future, even in a wilderness.

Then will He furnish food and drink, while time
mutates the planted seed to harvest? Life
so often breaks the heart of one who dreams.
You wrap yourself in silence, ears now deaf
to pleadings of a wife who loves . . . then go,
but go alone, without our sons and me.
I will return unto my father's land
a wife deserted, yet a princess, proud
of royal lineage. There I shall reside
and dream of when you shall come back . . . to me.

Two years later
Zipporah closed her eyes against the heat,
against the camel's sway across the sand
much like a boat upon the Persian Sea
which lapped the shores of home with cooling mists.
She uttered no complaint and held her back
correct and proud. One never knew when spies
from Moses' camp would sight their caravan,
and never would she have fatigue reflect
that she were humbled. Two long years had passed
since she returned to Midian to face
her father-priest's ungracious greeting; pride
soon festering before his scorn, regret
and loneliness becoming worse than claims
of righteous wife which Moses had denied,
and gradually her manly sons were filled
with strange remorse that they had missed the march
that led the Israelites from Egypt's land
and thus denied their place in Moses' plan
directing people through the sea while walls
of water held as stone so they might cross

on firm dry land, their father's staff held high.
Ah, what a sight . . . when Red Sea waters closed
in death around great Pharaoh's charioteers.
Such miracles had raced the wind in words
of wonderment. Her father hired a band
of Nomad spies to follow Moses' flock,
report their trek across the wilderness.
Yes, Jethro's house was well informed of all
the many miracles which proved her wrong,
and Jethro vowed Zipporah and her sons
should take their place with Moses, knowing not
if he would welcome them. Zipporah's heart,
an empty vessel filled with worried gloom . . .
her youth had vanished long ago, she felt
both frail and rootless like a dried out bush
of thistle. Soon the caravan must stop
for water, then she would get down and rest
inside the curtained litter, meanwhile hope
she would not faint into the darkness held
behind her eyes which had rejected glare
of sun. A coolness brushed her face, almost
as if a cloud had formed . . . perhaps the cloud
by day that sheltered all the Israelites . . .
new hope like eyelids of the morning stirred.
Zipporah looked upon the day now wrapped
in silvered coolness, Moses' camp entrenched
within a small oasis. Many friends
were rushing forth in welcome. Jethro now
embraced his son-in-law who greeted him
with pleasure, next his sons so straight and tall,
"Eliezer, Gershom, welcome home." He turned
to help his wife from kneeling camel, spoke

55

in tenderness. "Zipporah, you have come
at last." His arms were strong and somehow seemed
instilled with youth, then Miriam declared
the travelers had need of food and rest.
Her husband's sister led the way to one
large tent and told of past events since last
they met, new ways of life, their daily lot
of manna. Discontent had claimed a few . . .
who longed for such remembered edibles
as onions, melons, fresh Egyptian fish;
the fact that freedom always claimed its price
meant nothing now . . . they vowed that slavery
was not unbearable, when there was wine
to drink on festive days nor did they care
who ruled the land, for whether they must work
long days, or tramp the desert, life must end
the same, the body weary, little hope
for future wealth . . . they some way never felt
the joy, the inner peace that most of them
experienced in living as God willed.
By warming flame at night and shade by day
Jehovah had protected them . . . which proved
them still his chosen people. Miriam
seemed quite content . . . her beauty radiant.

Zipporah knew there was no turning back
that some way she must meet the challenge, prove
obedience, though fear, a wrinkled mask
of doubt would shadow her to mock each day,
almost a premonition that she lacked
the stamina for hardship yet survive.

Whatever happened . . . this was Destiny,
the strange dark suitor one must meet alone.

MARK OF FURY

Numbers 12:1,6-15

Flavius Josephus (A.D. 37 - A.D. 100), the noted Jewish Historian, gives the name and circumstances regarding the Ethiopian Princess whom Moses married.

MARK OF FURY

So now the ceremony was complete
and Tharbis, Ethiopian Princess,
took Moses' hand and walked toward the honor seat
beside their tent, a converted idolatress,
expecting homage from the Hebrews, turned
to face her husband graciously, she bowed
and presented keys to her fair city; spurned
the people's cold restraint and stood in proud
disdain. "My friends, through me, you now are safe
to pass through my vast lands. The oath is said!"

To Miriam her words could only chafe
the memory of dear Zipporah, dead
so little time of four past moons, a sad
small bird, brought back by irate father-king;
since when could wife leave husband? Should she add
insult to shame for all concerned, to cling
to personal demands? Moses gave
Zipporah, their two sons, and Jethro, all
a loving welcome, quickly called a slave
to tend their needs, though Zipporah seemed to pall
beneath relentless heat, for she was born
to coastal winds and Red Sea mists. In time,
as traveling went on, she grew forlorn,
her spirit wearied of the endless climb
of up and down across the dunes, and chose
the sleep of death to life. So now this dark
strange Princess enjoyed all royal status quos.

Thus Miriam spoke her mind to Aaron, "Mark
you well this fault, that God should only speak
to Moses. Am I not a prophetess as well?
Did not our women take their timbrels, seek
to follow me in dance, with songs to swell
in praise to God for our deliverance?
So now I prophecy . . . that Moses bought
much enmity as well as free expanse,
and soon the Israelites will face onslaught.
I do not trust this Ethiopian . . .
but look . . . the skies are growing black, they split
with fiery tongues of lightning, warning man
of God's displeasure. The sign is definite!
Hark Aaron, listen to the rising wind
and how it rages. Fear cuts through my heart,
let us go to the temple tent . . . it is I who have sinned,
my face is shamed at being called apart.
Come, Aaron, draw not back . . . why do you stare?
Come take my hand. OH GOD . . . my hands are white
with leprosy . . . the punishment of despair."

Now Moses stands by the pillar of fire, upright
with glory on his face. "Dear Moses, plead
for me. I cast myself in dust and weep
repenting tears. Forgive and intercede
to God for me who never shall know sleep
nor rest unless He cleanse my flesh. I know
that to speak against a chosen one I reap
of Satan's harvest. God has sentenced woe
of death upon my spirit. Now I wait
the verdict. Seven days you vow, must

I be shut outside the camp to meditate . . .
then again I may return. I go in trust,
and Praising God. My life, I consecrate."

A CORD OF SCARLET

Joshua 2:1-22
Joshua 6:17-23

Rahab, a celebrated woman of Jericho, who aided two soldiers sent out by Joshua to spy out the land.

Matthew 1:5 reveals that Rahab married Salmon, the son of Naasson, and thus she became a progenitor of the lineage of Jesus. Rahab was the mother of Boaz, Jesse's grandfather. Jesse was the father of David.

Knowing these historical facts, I have taken the liberty of making Salmon one of the spies that Rahab helped escape by a rope from the walls of Jericho.

A CORD OF SCARLET

The inn built on the wall of Jericho
was vacant just before the hour when trade
of dining and fellowship began. Rahab
now owned this place of beauty though she had paid
the price of harlot for lawful security.
She wished to dress before the evening's rush,
and started up the stairs when two strange men
burst through the door to plead in breathless hush,
"We are pursued. Would you hide us . . . we pay in gold."

They were Hebrew warriors, the kind that terrorized
the land, both young and strong, yet creatures trapped.
She motioned them to follow her, surmised
that should she refuse, a knife might pierce her heart,
for they were dedicated men to a cause
in following their Jehovah's leading. Upstairs
they heard gruff voices below that quoted laws
for those who harbored spies. She pointed to steps
that led to the roof where stalks of grain were placed
to dry. "Here! Cover yourselves with flax and wait."

She returned to the inn to supervise and faced
with calm a captain of the cavalry.
"Two Hebrew spies you say! I never dreamed
our enemy was within the city walls . . .
two strangers came but left at dusk which seemed
but wise, since the gates will soon be closed. Pursue
them now and you will capture both . . . make haste."
She watched the soldiers leave and welcomed guests
arriving. She loitered awhile before she retraced

her steps to the roof where one man still reclined
beneath the flax. The younger gazing entranced
upon the lighted torches of Jericho
that blended people with flickering shadows which danced
in happy unconcern of threatening attack.
He turned and smiled as Rahab's heart felt pain
of strange regret that she was what she was . . .
his gaze made her feel of special clay with no stain
of commonness. His voice was low, "This wall
not only protects the city, its width a vault
of treasure." She nodded, "You have figured well,
though no doubt our people face a Hebrew assault.
Yes we have heard how you march across the land
and how your God delivers all to you
in battle, until opposing warriors are struck
with awe. I tremble that I have let you view
details of Jericho's defense . . . but yet
I believe in the Hebrew God and would like to hear
how one, such as I, approaches Him. Perhaps
there is no consideration in His sphere
of justice, for a gentile who wishes to change
her existence." She soon was telling this young man,
named Salmon, about her aged parents and all
her brothers and sisters, and how their care began
for her, the eldest child, who must run the inn . . .
and how it seemed so simple to grant a few
requests in return for burdens lifted . . . He brushed
her words away by telling her that he knew
Jehovah judged and forgave the repentant heart,
that through confession, salvation was granted each
who changed their ways and worshipped Him. There
    seemed

much more to say but silence weighed as stone
while thought took wing to the place of wishful dreams.

The second warrior roused himself and said,
"The moon is high and we must leave to resume
our mission." She nodded. "Those who sought you were
    led
toward the Jordan, so travel the other way and hide
in the mountains until our spies give up and return.
Now come and see the way of escape, but first
I bargain . . . that when your army comes to burn
this city, as they have others in their wake,
that you will spare my family and me
and that your people accept us with kindly hearts."

They pledged their word. "We grant you clemency."

"Then come." She led them to her room where she kept
five fathoms of rope composed of scarlet flax
which she had braided thick. "I keep it here
in case of fire. At the base of the wall, haystacks . . .
swing through the window and lower yourself, the rope
secured to this bolted ring, and when you fall
into the hay you will be hidden from sight,
but stay there until the city sleeps, then crawl
in shadow toward the east where lies a ridge
of rocks which will camouflage and protect from foes."

The eldest warrior grasped the rope and edged
across the sill as Salmon spoke, "When you close
the inn tonight, retrieve this scarlet cord
and decorate your windows in such a way

that none surmise it as a sign to us,
that our own soldiers make no mistake and betray
our oath." Then suddenly he took her hand,
"Do not have misgivings, Rahab . . . we shall arrive,
remember our ways are different, but a life
much better than this for you and yours, so strive
for patience. Now farewell until we meet
again before too long." Then one quick leap
and he was going down through shadows, dark
and silent, while Rahab learned she still could weep . . .
then soon a phantom bird trilled low to tell
that they were free. Then sounded a trumpet-call
to assure old Jericho that all was well . . .
the city could sleep in peace. She began to haul
the rope inside and think how she might drape
the windows with scalloped edge, as the plot took shape.

MOMENT OF DECISION

Judges 4:9

Biblical history remains as Deborah prophecied to Barak,* that if he insisted she go into battle with him that the victory would not be to his honor but placed into the hands of a woman who trusted God.

* Bā´rak

MOMENT OF DECISION

Young Deborah sat beneath the palm to wait
for Barak, the ranking warrior who could lead
the Israelites against the advancing foe
except he felt their land was doomed by fate
before iron chariots whose lightning speed
descending like a plague, against hand-made bow
and spear of an untrained army. Deborah knew
he doubted, yet she was a chosen one, with gift
of mystic sight, with sound inside her ear,
which came from God. Her eyes gazed over blue
tinged valleys through prophetic haze that shift
the future into now. With vision clear
she saw herself on horseback riding within
a sheath of smoke all filled with acrid smell
of danger, along a pathway between the dark
and sudden thunder, mocking the battle's din
while ten strong tribes fought bravely beneath the spell
of courage, shown by a woman with valiant spark
of faith, yet Deborah shuddered at the sight
of blood and death, the sacrifice of few
to save the life of many, they giving all . . .
and yet it must be so, until the flight
of the Canaanites. She must not judge, but view
her place in time as one proclaimed to enthrall
with singing, the victory as the foe should flee . . .
Now vision faded. She spoke as Barak drew near,
"Go Barak, take with thee ten thousand strong,
speak not . . . I know you will not advance without me . . .
you think my presence will keep men from showing fear
. . . so I shall go before them with destiny's song.

73

SHADOWED DESTINY

Judges 16:1-30

The prowess of Samson is told in very few verses in the Bible but there are historic facts behind the story. The Philistines, in an attempt to expand their territory eastward, had penetrated into the land of Judah. During this clash between the countries, Samson, a judge and leader of his people, would be more than eager to find out something of the enemy's strategies. What better way than through a beautiful woman?

All indicates that Delilah was a spy and both she and Samson were involved in intrigue, he playing a game at letting her call the guards to take him and she believing it impossible to overpower him, until both of them were surprised and defeated through misunderstanding.

In part three of *Shadowed Destiny* there is no scriptural confirmation that Delilah was in the temple when Samson destroyed it. However in *Judges 16:27* we are told three thousand people had filled the rooftop of the temple. To conclude that Delilah attended this great festival seems only natural and logical, since she played the leading role in placing Samson in the hands of his enemy.

SHADOWED DESTINY

Delilah:
Arise slave, inform the captain of the guard
that Delilah has turned the hourglass; tell him make haste
else Samson, Judge of Judea, shall soon bombard
the palace, expecting the favor of being placed
beside me, as honored guest, at my new-moon-feast.
Show this man out, Hadassah, then help me dress.

Tonight I shall wear my opals brought from the east
of Ophir. Maid, use the complexion tints with finesse;
pale lips, soft shadowed eyelids. Let me appear
beguiling, ready to follow love. The veil
across my shoulders must be phantom-sheer,
as mist that floats through oasis palms, as pale
as moon-brushed pomegranate blossoms. These long
    earrings
should be filled with lotus perfume, while the subtle blue
of my dress, the impression of twilight haze that clings
above a river.
       Now the captain is due,
escort him here, so we may speak alone.

Sire, you were waiting. My pardon! I should have known.

Captain:
You look divine, Delilah, though a bit
naive for the siren of Sorek Valley. Perchance
our feminine spy has met her match; must admit
the man of Judea suspects her feigned romance;
is amused at her moods of chameleon changes, her skills

to deceive him, a judge from beyond the northern hills.
Thrice he has tricked you. Have you some excuse?
Or do you enjoy a clandestined game of truce?

Delilah:
I disregard your insult. Your sentries, at length
have stood behind those pillars where they could hear
his riddles, his tales of superhuman strength,
and how I acted the play, made each movement appear
steeped in admiration. When he slept
I tied green withes, new ropes, and braids of hair
to bind his arms, then whispered a warning, and wept
that soldiers would capture him, lest he break the snare
I had invented in jest. Then I trembled, lay prone
at his feet, and watched him shake off slumber, snap
his girdings, as guardsmen slithered away. To attone
I took my lyre, began to sing, to enwrap
a ballad about the mighty Samson. I teased
his vanity, sang of a peacock that looked with disdain
at lesser fowls of the courtyard who seldom pleased
the spectators, having no fan to spread. The refrain
extolled the bird's cunning. It wasn't easy to laugh
and pretend my part was but frolic. Adrift
in his steel-like arms my heart quivered. I was half
afraid he might destroy me, but he was swift
to respond with trust, to this make-believe, while I
became the one who was trapped. Now I complain,
for I am convinced all plots will go awry . . .

Sire, I can do no more. It is best we conclude
our contract . . . bring to an end this interlude.

Captain:
Your words are those of a maiden who lies awake
to follow the moon across the arch of heaven;
denying reason in restless watching for break
of dawn; bewildered at sadness that seems to leaven
old hatreds. You wish on stars and sigh in your pillow!
Delilah, you are a woman; with Samson this vice
is his weakness. So sing as the nightingale in the willow
to soothe the strong man's suspicion; pay the price
which the wheel of fortune casts. This is my advice.

Delilah:
The decision is yours, Sire. Still Samson has cast a spell
of indulgence upon the land. The people view
this demi-god of strength with wonder. The bell
of fate has not struck for his doom as yet. His debut
in yesterday's tournament, came when a wild
black stallion had thrown our finest riders, then came
the chant, "Let Samson tame him!", starting mild
and swelling to clamor. Samson let the flame
of excitement spread until the judges rose
and asked if he cared to try.
                            He stood and bowed,
became the image of valor caught in the throes
of circumstance, a stag held poised and proud,
scenting the hounds, yet sure as an eagle perched
on unattained peak to survey the world.
Samson removed his toga, quickly searched
the arena; timed his jump. The stallion whirled

to eye his foe. What a sight to watch! Each took
the other's measure, vied for advantage, gripped
in tension. Samson moved, the black devil shook
his mane in warning. Samson adroitly flipped
a stone to detract his attention, then sprang on his back
and clasped his throat. White bands clutched ebony wind
that lashed and stormed against this human attack.
The crowd grew still as Samson disciplined
the ebb and flow of the tempest. Slowly he gained
the trust of the foaming beast . . . it slackened its pace,
and gradually, pranced with pride.
                                        As master he reined
the stallion before the judges, turned his face
to the cheering crowd.
                        Now my Captain, do you care
to destroy the people's idol? Do you dare?
Too hot a flame could consume the avenger. Think twice
before you rub the flint of sacrifice.

Captain:
I marvel that you, the exotic flower of night,
now yearn for warmth of sun beneath the spray
of compassion! The hour is too late to become contrite.
Remember the double fee you received as pay,
eleven hundred pieces of silver pound.
Our contract is valid. By your own terms you are bound.
Delilah, your guests arrive. Let joy resound.

80

PART II

Delilah:
This night will remain a lasting memory,
it was paced like a spinning disc of lottery.
Now the sound of chariot wheels grow dim. The last guest
has departed. My ears still ring with revelry . . .
soon dawn shall tinge with flame the earth's far crest
and shepherds' lutes will echo with sorcery
across the valley. Listen! Hear their plea
as if the gods were weeping at our plight.
Ah, Samson, how much longer can we flee
reality? It is best we leave this country.
Consent, sheer your flowing locks, subject
identity and blend with the crowd, so none will suspect.

Samson:
Delilah, no. Wherever we go, my power
will defend you. I fear no man, and my hair is a mark
of distinction. Now relax my pretty flower.
Fret not, come rest while the night still holds the dark.
Delilah, you fill me with delight. I've known
of your situation, wondered when you'd break
beneath the tides of deception's sea, atone
before the flame of love. It is time to forsake
all pretense between the two of us. Let me stroke
your hair where sapphire shadows lurk; your eyes
are rain-kissed pools of jet. Your lips provoke
the fires of intrigue as does your every guise.
Be still, for we shall laugh in fortune's face,
in time your people may call me friend, with grace.
So long as I do not sheer this hair, my force

of strength will endure. Let the Philistines seek the source
in vain. Now sleep, my arms your resting place.

Delilah:
Samson, how easily you shed anxiety
to sleep, reposed and beautiful, though my plan
is best, and while you think your dignity
depends on your hair, I now shall ring for the man
who barbers the courtiers' hair.
                                        Enter quietly, slave,
work lightly, with care, as you trim and shape the head
of my lord Samson, while I croon and gently wave
my fan to cool his brow.
                                'Tis done. Now tread
with silent feet as you leave.
                                        My love, how strange
you look to me, yet still handsome with the change.
Now I shall act out our comedy of pretense.
"Awaken, lest warriors find Samson without defense!"

Samson:
Ah Delilah, you startled me. I slept in sound
peacefulness. My eyes are still heavy. Great God!
my hair is shaven! You fool! Now that you have found
the hour to transform the man to common clod
are you satisfied? Last night I trusted you . . .
like a naive schoolboy I let you strip me of all
my wisdom. Now I must escape! Must pursue
the life of homeless wanderer, lest I fall
beneath the sword of my enemy. Do you know
what you have done or can you, at will, erase
all expression of guilt? Perhaps you should taste of woe

82

with me. Perhaps experience one last embrace
wherein love becomes a death mask of passion's face.

Delilah:
No! Samson! Have you gone mad? Stay where you are!
I swear I meant you no great harm, but now
your face is white with hostility. You mar
the love that we have known. One move and I vow
I shall call the guards.
                    Ah Samson, forgive me . . . please . . .
I knew not that you felt so strongly about your hair.
My dear, it will grow out soon, so do not tease
Delilah. This small thing could not impair
your strength. Do you expect me to really believe
such foolishness?
                    Very well, I'll play your game . . .
I'll call the sentries and again watch them heave
while they try to hold you, watch you shame
our strongest soldiers, proud of battle acclaim.
Guards!

Samson:
Be still, you woman of Satan! I swear I shall not
let you drag me to disgrace by your sinister plot!

Delilah:
Guards! My love, you were not quick enough
to catch me, though I no longer fear your bluff.
Guards! The mighty Samson's hair is shorn
his vitality gone . . . he is now undone.
There! Take him, soldiers.

Samson! do not scorn
my acting. Now! Samson, break away . . .
Great god Dagon! His stamina IS gone . . .
Samson the strong, the legend, the paragon . . .
they drag him off in chains like lightning-felled tree!
Ah woe is me! He spoke the truth and I
was not convinced, but neither could I foresee
this web of doom.
                              God Dagon, I wish to die!
How they will torture him before he is slain!
Oh God, if there is a God, I can't stand the pain
of this blind mistake, one I can not rectify.
I have destroyed all meaning to life! Let me die!

PART III

Delilah:
Regret had lived with her a year, and loss
of Samson had intensified, her days
a brambled path of thorns. Delilah's cross
of loneliness withered joy, and life a daze
of pretense. She was a captive of her own
intrigue. Life meant so little, yet she fought
to live. She wondered why, for she had grown
much like a wasp that few friends seldom sought.
And now today, the Philistines had planned
a festival to Dagon, praising him
for delivering Samson into their hand,
and she, Delilah, to be honored. This grim
facetiousness of fate had torn old scars
apart, though she had steeled herself to endure

the eyes of curiosity and let stars
arrange events. Her escort had come to insure
a proper entrance to the seat reserved,
where she could see them lead blind Samson in.
Some way she must remain aloof, she observed
the boisterous crowd, though sound began to din
within her ears, as did her guilt. The place
was overflowing . . . they said three thousand jammed
the rooftop, waiting in the sun. No space
was left at all and those outside had rammed
the doors for entrance. Now the trumpets blared,
then silence hung like doom till the people saw
the enemy, whose sightless eyes but stared
toward what he heard, then came a roaring guffaw.
Her mouth began to fill with gall, her breath
a tortured pain. Oh how she hated them
who had burned away his sight. She wished that death
would claim them all. Yet what right had she to condemn!

Now Samson spoke to the lad who held his chain . . .
together they eased between the pillars. There
he took his stand and suddenly seemed to regain
his former strength as excitement charged the air.
Her pulsing heart contracted . . . she rose in wonder . . .
his hair was grown long again . . . and now he threw
his might against the pillars which cracked like thunder.
The multitudes, alarmed, began to spew
out oaths, as guards rushed forth with spears to slay
the mighty Samson before it was too late;
but now the power of his Jehovah lay
confusion as people ran . . . but every gate
refused to open. The temple began to lean . . .

in blinding flash their fate she could foresee,
she stood and watched the giant's straining back.
In strange exhileration she felt a degree
of triumph while the people screamed and tried
to find escape . . . trampling, pushing in vain.
She called that she was there, above the tide,
"Wait, Samson . . . together we shall die!" A rain
of crumbling mortar sifted down . . . he turned
his sightless eyes as if he'd heard her cry . . .
and then the temple slowly collapsed, and churned
defeat with victory . . . his last reply.

THE RUBY SEAL

Book of Ruth

Ruth, a Moabite, married first, Mahlon, the son of Naomi. Ruth's second marriage was to Boaz, a relative of her first husband.

Ruth's and Boaz' son was Obed, the father of Jesse, who was the father of David.

Since Boaz was the son of Salmon and Rahab, Ruth becomes the daughter-in-law of Rahab in her second marriage.

Book of Ruth — 4:7 - - - concerning the last line of the poem.

. . . for to confirm all things; a man plucked off his shoe, and gave it to his neighbor; and this was a testimony in Israel.

THE RUBY SEAL

The sisters turned away from two new graves,
the scent of flowers, finger like, impressed
each fold of garment, penetrating hair
and nostrils, almost sickening in strength.
Behind dark widow veils, hot tears escaped
for they must soon decide which fork of road
to take. Both Ruth and Orpah had been marked
with barrenness of child to bind the ties
of Israel, their husband's kinsmen free
of care for them by law. Thus they were told
to now return unto their father's house.
An evil wind of trouble blew across
the valley, cold with fear, for both had once
denounced the god of Moab, had embraced
Jehovah, great and only God of truth.

At home, in meekness, Orpah packed her clothes.
How could she turn her back on life, appease
old gods? Ruth vowed to cast herself before
Naomi, Mahlon's mother . . . whither thou
must goest, I will go . . . your God my God.

Ten moons had come and gone in Bethlehem,
and barley season soon would end, so Ruth
must turn her gleaning next to wheat. She worked
to care for both Naomi and herself,
both knew the face of poverty . . . and yet
Naomi's husband had possessed vast lands
that now were waste, until some kinsman would
redeem the old estates through purchase, else

embrace the youngest widow as his wife,
but Ruth, a Moabite, was looked upon
as some strange blossom, one of foreign blood
by men of Bethlehem. Now, God had led
her toward the fields of Boaz, a man of wealth
and honor. He had asked his servants who
the sun bronzed maiden was and bade them let
her reap without annoyance, carry all
she wished. Naomi smiled and spoke wise words,
"Tonight, you must adorn yourself and go
quite late where Boaz winnows barley, cast
yourself before this kinsman . . . beauty will
awaken him to where his duty lies."

Obedience surmounting fear, Ruth walked
alone, with moonlight flung across her path
to point the way toward distant shed. She wore
a gown reserved for days of festive note,
then draped a veil of thin blue haze across
her hair and face. In darkest hour she felt
secure beneath annointing wings of faith,
else shame and pride would turn her steps away.

Deep sleep had claimed the reapers, every one,
and Ruth slipped quietly to Boaz' mat,
to lay beside his feet and wait until
first weariness should lift. With trembling heart
she touched his ankle. Boaz, wide awake,
beheld a moon-wrapped woman, eyes aflame,
heard words of sorrow's plight. He studied her
and listened with his inner ear to hear
the nightingale above a fountained pool . . .

he touched her cheek before he covered her
from view. "I know thou art both virtuous
and beautiful . . . above rare rubies held
within my palm. Tomorrow I shall do
that which the law requires, to bind the trust
of thine inheritance, demand the seal,
exchange of shoe before all eyes . . . for thee."

PROMISE OF BITTER ROOT

I Samuel 1:1-28
I Samuel 2:18-20

Hannah, faithful to her oath
in giving her son back to the source
of life, God blessed her with three sons
and two daughters.

PROMISE OF BITTER ROOT

The child was walking sure
on his chubby two year legs
and he was weened, so now
the day of reckoning had come
for Hannah to keep her promise
to the Lord Jehovah.

On that day of dedication
three years ago, she had gone
with her husband and his other wife,
the mother of sons and daughters,
to the temple-sacrificing
though her heart had been filled with envy
mixed with sad humiliation
at being childless.

She recalled that day so vividly,
the desert fluttered like a bride
beneath a pallid sky washed clean
from sudden shower that had brought forth
cactus flowers until it seemed
that all the world was productive
except her body within life's purpose
that of being a woman,
complete and fulfilled.

Nothing had seemed so terrible
to her then, as the shame of barrenness
so she had made her holy promise
and witnessed her grief before Elie, the priest,

that should God favor her with a man child
she would lend him back to serve
in the temple all the days of his life.

How fast the time had passed
for she knew a greater torment now . . .
the oath she gave must be fulfilled . . .
her eyes misted as she watched Samuel
examining a small green leaf . . .
she smoothed his little tunic
and took his muscular baby hand.

All the way up the hill
he talked of camels, birds, and the three
sacrificial bullocks led by servants . . .
it did not matter to the child
that his mother walked in silence,
he was entranced with everything
along the way.

Soon they approached the temple,
its shadow stretching long and cool
as she rang the entrance bell to ask
for audience with Elie, the priest,
who was expecting them.

Hannah set her basket down,
filled with gifts, an ephod of flour
and a bottle of rare old wine . . .
the priest came hurrying in flowing robes
to welcome them and presented
Samuel with tree-ripe figs

so that the boy hardly noticed
her kiss and touch upon his hair . . .
    "I know he will be happy here.
    Each year, I shall make him a little coat
    and bring it at the time
    of sacrifice."

Hannah watched them walking
down the garden path . . .
she turned and ran to nearest tree
to hide behind the trunk,
to lay her cheek on the splintery bark and sob,
    "Forgive me, God, for these mother's tears.
    Thou granted me my heart's desire
    that left me with leanness of soul . . .
    tonight, Lord, I beseech thee,
    make little boy Samuel so sleepy
    he will not miss his mother's kiss
    and tucking him in for the night.
    Have mercy, Lord, though I know
    you care for your own."

MILK WITH MY WINE

I Kings 1:1-53
I Kings 2:1-25

Abishag arouses the interest and curiosity more than any other woman in the scriptures, perhaps because so little is written about her.

According to William S. Smith's *Bible Dictionary*: Abishage, beautiful Shunammite from Shunem, in the tribe of Issachar, taken into David's harem to comfort him in his old age but whom he "knew not." *(I Kings 1:1-14)*

Shunem, the native home of Abishag is mentioned by Eusebius (Ecclesiastical historian) as five miles south of Mount Tabor and then known as *Sulem*.

If Shulem and Shunem are equivalent we may conjecture that the Shulammite, the object of Solomon's passion, was Abishag, the most lovely girl of her day and at the time of David's death, the most prominent person in Jerusalem.

Adonijah, the eldest son of King David, born of Haggith, also loved Abishag who may have favored him over Solomon. Could Adonijah be the lost lover of the Shulammite in *Songs of Solomon*? Is Abishag, in the last four stanzas of the book calling to Adonijah? Perhaps appealing for his life?

Adonijah expected to take over the kingdom at his father's death. He was prepared to do so, and the kingdom was divided in feeling between the two sons. David, however, favoring Bathsheba, his lifetime love, promised her that Solomon, their son, should be anointed king. Adonijah, when he learned of the anointing, accepted the fact but lost no time in requesting Abishag, the Shunammite, for his bride.

Solomon, in anger refused, standing on a legal technicality, that any advance upon the harem was an attack upon the throne, though a king's command could have adjusted the matter. He ordered the death penalty for his half-brother, Adonijah. Why did Solomon refuse to give up this one woman out of a harem of many hundred? Did Abishag have anything to say about it? Did she remain in the harem? Did Bathsheba, in jealousy of both husband and son, see to it that Abishag's name was removed from all court records? The reader wonders what became of Abishag.

MILK WITH MY WINE

Young Abishag the Shunammite had wept
through endless nights since coming here. Still tense
with dread she stood resigned to fate, observed
court regents checking sundials while they kept
attendants rushing with expedience.

Her flesh was rubbed with cassia oil, reserved
for cherished concubines, eyes tinged with woad,
and lips enhanced with safflower. Servants brought
the bridal robe, a trailing cloud of white
adorned with pearls and crystal flecks that glowed
as crescents. Abishag turned wings of thought
toward home where days were filigree delight,
where she once played her harp, creating song
within the garden walls for family.

One day a sun-bronzed soldier stopped to buy
a calf to serve his army camped along
the hillcrest. While he talked, flame suddenly
enwrapped them both, though neither dare defy
tradition. Neither spoke, though eyes had met
across her father's shoulder, interchanged
magnetic favor. When the moon turned full
he came as Adonijah, Prince-Vedette
of Israel, whose horsemen often ranged
the land, for he was held responsible
for welfare of people. How she tried to tame
her anguished heart, a wild caged bird undone
by striking wings on golden bars that cleaved
their world apart. Why should the prince acclaim

103

her beauty's lure above comparison?
Her father spoke, for he was not deceived,
and knew that heirs to thrones could seldom choose
a mate, unless two empires should unite,
and this a boyish king dare not refuse.
"My daughter, like the shepherdess who turned
her sheep in coves where stormy winds were slight,
must guard the entrance lest it be a snare."

Bold Adonijah chose a paraphrase,
"For such a shepherdess most any man
would watch the flock with her, protect the lair
at night and wish on comets when they blaze."

For weeks a moody Abishag would scan
the stars, review her heritage, acclaimed
with noble blood. Small wonder she was fired
with strange anticipation when one day
three envoys from the court appeared, and named
the virgin Abishag as one desired
for Israel's king. They read without delay
a mandate filled with praise and placed a chain
of gold about her throat.
                              Then she defied
the couriers, who thought her fires might move
the ailing king to warmth and stay his pain.
Physicians felt such spirit could provide
a stimulant and health would thus improve.
And so they brought her here.
                              Now trumpets blared
from palace walls with festive note. A maid
began to dress her hair in coronet

of jet black braids, another ayah flared
her skirt a bit, and hope began to fade
as fear devised a bloodless statuette.
The harem veils were draped with care until
her beauty was concealed, and only eyes
could see. They led her toward the great façade
now thronged with people. Abishag stood still
to gain composure. None must criticise
the Shunammite, consider her a clod
when matched against Bathsheba's charm. If fate
had placed the stars, then she would wangle fame
and rule behind the throne.
                                    Now tambourines
and choruses began to emulate
her virtue. Now the people must proclaim
her eminence. With all inherent means
of grace she made her entrance manifest
a goddess. Poised with pride she viewed the guards
who held the crowds aside while the maidens threw
rose petals for her feet. Her gaze possessed
hypnotic luster . . . subjects knelt as cards
blown down before the wind, as was her due.

At farthest end of hall two massive doors
screened court nobility of every rank,
the king would take her hand, then both would leave,
so feasting might begin and troubadours
could toast their happiness. Her courage sank . . .

Oh why, cruel Adonijah, did you weave
this web? You plotted all for me and I

will not forget. Revenge will still be mine,
for often we shall meet within these walls.

Some day you will seek my favor. I shall lie,
insist remembrance fades . . . drink milk with wine . . .
and listen to your cry as darkness falls.

II

Four days later:

Above the screened roofgarden, wispy clouds
adorned mauve skies, the wishing star hung blurred
through tears as Abishag sung whispered psalms
to chords she strummed upon a harp. The crowds
had feasted, then had gone their way, when word
was sent that virgin charms had failed. Now qualms
began to flare concerning Israel's king,
whose royal hand secured the kingdom. Fear,
the beggar lice of quandary, spread afar
to wait in strange unrest, an unseen thing
that Abishag now sensed, yet with sincere
devotion to her lord whose angular
frail body lay in deepest sleep. As nurse
she begged for quietness, and all complied.
They knew she calmed the king with music . . . dreams
for each were fused with yesterdays. In verse
she fashioned thought and mourned her shattered pride
that she remained a virgin bride. Her schemes
for power now lay in shambles.

As she sang
she was aware that someone lurked behind
the lattice. Who would dare to spy! She turned
with steady gaze and Adonijah sprang
before her.

       "Do not scream! Must I remind
the Shunammite that love has ever burned
within my troubled heart. Sweet Abishag,
please listen . . . do not back away. One sound
upon the gong and you have sealed my death.

Below my stallion waits with saddlebag
supplied with needs until my head is crowned
as king. I swear to you, with truth's pure breath,
the army waits with Joab at the helm.
Abiathar, the prophet loved by all
the people since the days he brought the Ark
of Covenant to rest within the realm
of David, joins our cause and will enthrall
the multitude, who knows that now the dark
pursuer waits to claim their king, my own
beloved father.

       Abishag, believe
that I made not the plan to bring you here,
that councilors of court decide for throne
and country. Lovely maidens ever weave
their legends, heard by every cavalier
who roams the kingdom. Now you understand."

"Enough, Prince Adonijah! Shame should stain
your face to strike against your father. True,
his days are but a vapored lotus-land

where lemures wait patiently. Restrain
ambition . . . angels soon will lead him through
gray Lethe mist. As yet his mind sometimes
has clear remembrance.
                              Wait and let us ask
his blessing. He has been so kind to think
of me as daughter, calls me Tamar, rhymes
his words around her life. The king should bask
in warm affection while the shadowed brink
draws near . . . and we should then have no regret."

"You make it sound so simple, yet I vow
this land is cleaved into, each hour a cloud
that gathers doom for us. Do not forget
that Solomon stands ready to endow
himself with royal scepter. Some have bowed
before him even as I tarry here
yet neither could I leave without a pledge
to you, my Abishag. Four hours I paced
the outer rim beside the wall in fear
for you. My brother stood beside the edge
of vine-wrapped lattice, spied, as eyes embraced
the Shunammite. He listened to your song
as though each word had stirred his heart with need,
yet daring not the risk of peril, left
the field. Thus I am here though I prolong
the thinnest thread of fortune which can lead
to victory. My spirit lies bereft
of joy without the love of Abishag."

"My faith has been restored, my heart is stirred
with rapture, ever will it follow you . . .

contain yourself, beloved.
                              Would you drag
all honor through the dust? It is absurd
to mock the fates who grant which souls are due,
and apprehension flutters in my veins
for both of us. Your desperate plan to save
your heritage from Solomon, my course
a pawn between the two of you, remains
a battle still unfought.
                              My love I gave
to you since first we met, without remorse.
Make haste, my Adonijah, stars adjourn
and soon the palace starts the day. The king
grows restless in his sleep. I place a kiss
with fingertips upon your lips. Return
in glory is my prayer, else the sting
of sorrow draws me toward death's nemesis.
Farewell, dear Adonijah! "
                              Fear runs cold
and chokes my breath! His muffled footsteps grow
more dim, though danger haunts my peace. I dream
of him who lives as shepherd with his fold
of valiant soldiers. Patience now, I owe
his majesty, who wakens, my esteem.

"You rested well, my lord, for dawn grows pale,
and vassals brought tree-ripened apricots
to tempt your appetite . . . let me adjust
your pillows, bathe your face."
                                    He seems more frail!
Ah, Adonijah, bring your patriots
soon now. In God, and in your love, I trust.

109

The king is weakening. I throw a kiss
upon the wind to touch your lips, return
lest sorrow draws me toward death's nemesis.

THORNS OF VIRTUE

I Kings 2:13-25

Bathsheba, the old queen, must have resented the beautiful Abishag, the young concubine taken to her husband's quarters to nurse him in his last hours. Did she resent the Shunammite's influence on her son, Solomon? Did she suspect that Abishag was in love with Adonijah rather than the annointed king?

Bathsheba appears over-eager to assist Prince Adonijah in his request for Abishag by going to Solomon in person to appeal his cause. One wonders if Bathsheba had anything to do with striking Abishag's name from all possible records so that she would become lost to history.

THORNS OF VIRTUE

Bathsheba, looking down into the vast
and busy courtyard, watched the gardeners weed
the flower beds, and irrigate fruit trees,
prune shrubbery, flush fountains, clean the pool
of lotus lilies, plucking yellowed leaves
lest they should turn to slime. The mounted guard
patrolled the castle, checking palace gates,
as tradesmen brought their wares, and paused to eye
the swaying hips of water maids, enroute
from springs, with balanced jar upon their head.
So many years this scene had filled her heart
with peace and sweet content; but now a black
depression withered her. Bathsheba knew
her lord, King David, hovered near the edge
of consciousness, swayed in and out of strength,
to puzzle all physicians. Thus they grasped
at straws in shrewd analysis, until
in desperation, hatched the plot to bring
a young and lovely concubine to him,
to share his bed, and stir his pulse with warmth.

The stupid fools had barred Bathsheba, known
to be the favored queen, the cherished wife,
from royal chambers. Not so many years
ago their love had rocked the country, brought
the prophet's curse upon their heads, though fire
of wonder fused their star within the storm.

The scene below became a reverie,
a village in her homeland, that of Dan,

a clan whose source went back to Jacob's time
when he created, through his sons, twelve tribes
of Israel. Bathsheba was aware
that Abishag walked proudly too, as kin
of Issachar, an equal heritage.
So now, she dare not scorn the Shunammite's
exotic beauty, vibrant, golden-hued,
a rare and precious blossom from the moon
which captivated two of David's sons.
Her Solomon, and Adonijah born
of Haggith, both sought favor from the maid,
stood waiting from afar til one of them
should sit upon the throne of Israel.

This moment Adonijah's army camped
in yonder hills, believing he was heir,
as eldest prince, to Israel's crown, and all
the king's possessions. What a stark surprise
for Adonijah when he learned his loss!
Her Solomon had gone with Priests Zodak
and Nathan, by decree of David, down
to Gihon, just outside Jerusalem,
to be annointed king. Bathsheba's heart
had known that David's pledge to her was sealed
by love which few could ever know on earth.
With Solomon as king, her place remained
secure within the palace. Even so
this maid from Shunem was a threat to her
from hidden corners. Solomon was blind
to facts, though Abishag had not disguised
her love for Adonijah, even talked
of him as princely shepherd-boy who lived

afar and waited there for her to come.
She never dreamed Bathsheba knew of whom
she meant. Poor Solomon preferred to think
that Abishag but chose to taunt, pretend
a suitor; nor had Abishag been pleased
with songs that Solomon composed and sang
in praise of one fair rose of Sharon, one
to whom he gave his heart and soul, and laid
the kingdom at her feet. Her smile was cold,
her fragile casualness, the rope of hemp
that bound the future king to her small whims.
Bathsheba's wisdom bid her act with slow
deliberation where the Shunammite
held power. Also, there were those at court
who plotted evil things against the Queen,
Bathsheba. They remembered early years
when she was still the swarthy Hittite's wife,
when David saw her in the garden, built
upon the roof and sent a slave to bring
her to the palace. David learned the truth,
that she was but a pawn, so pledged in truce
of war, to spare her people. Hittites stemmed
from Heth, the second son of Cainan, cursed
by Israel's God, and she, Bathsheba, cringed
each time Uriah touched her flesh. Thus he
had found no satisfaction in their state
of marriage. Why, she wondered, did she think
of days so long ago when she was young,
a burnished blaze that flared in David's soul,
a counterpart of being, felt by both,
enwrapt within the web of destiny.

115

The trumpets sounded suddenly, to call
the people from their work. Bathsheba watched
them look toward Nathan standing on the steps
before the palace. Solomon was there
behind him, waiting. Now the prophet raised
his arms, "King David chooses Solomon
to sit upon the kingdom's throne." He knelt
before the youth and kissed the royal ring.
The people echoed salutations, bowed
with praise before their sovereign Lord and King.

So now Prince Adonijah would be forced
to seek the temple's sanctuary, plead
for mercy from his brother, Solomon,
who would in kindness soon forgive, and grant
him liberty, if he but swear an oath
of loyalty to king and Israel.
Bathsheba smiled in contemplation. Soon
Prince Adonijah would request his place
be reestablished in the court, perhaps
would ask one favor. Surely Solomon
who owned the royal harems, plus the wealth
of all the kingdom, surely he would grant
one maid, whose status was quite different
from all the rest, this nurse and concubine
whom David never claimed as bride, one called
the Shunammite. Bathsheba visualized
how it would be. Yes, she could wait, abide
her time, until she dare expose the wiles
of Abishag. Then Solomon would see
the maid's deceitfulness and send her forth.

Though thorns of jealousy would shatter pride
he'd praise his mother for her shrewd insight.
Thus she, Bathsheba would be rid of her
who held priority, yet mocked her son.

How wise to work through Adonijah, tempt
him with the burning dream of Abishag
who languished for her one and only love.
Indeed, Bathsheba could afford to wait.

THE STARS HAVE CHOSEN

I Kings 10:1-13

The Queen of Sheba is given no name in Scripture. A new insight was revealed by the *National Geographic*: Vol. 138, No. 6, page 856 (December 1970), stating that Emperor Haile Selassie I counts himself the 225th ruler of the lineage of King Solomon of Israel and Queen Makeda, through their son Menelik.

THE STARS HAVE CHOSEN

The rooftop garden lay in shadowed dusk
as wind flowed through the torchiere flames that cast
a mellow light across the woman's face.
Her quill brought life to papyrus, drawing close
a distant land where love, once lived, became
a certain kind of prism, such that one
must enter into, so to understand.
She chose her words bestowed as precious gems,
for words could blow old embers back to flame
or snuff them out, to lie in acrid ash.

> My warmest greeting, noble Solomon . . .
> Each night since leaving Israel my thoughts
> return to you as homing birds. The moon
> cast beams of magic over loneliness
> and distance, as our lives must ever be
> who rule two countries. Heartache often shares
> the bed of royalty and stalks the path
> of proud existence. Often barren sand
> will grow exotic flowers tough of root,
> though you, my lord, desire new buds of strange
> extraction. Now it seems miraculous
> that we should dare to touch a comet's fire
> and live to part. Yet, noble king, your wise
> advice secured my crown, for nevermore
> shall councils stress a foreign marriage pact
> and have me share my throne. My caravan
> reached homeland after nine full moons were past
> when stars divined a living bond to bind
> my heart to Solomon. Our son was born
> a week ago, a wondrous child of strength

121

and beauty, fused with time and destiny.
His name is Menelik, the heir and king
of Ethiopia. My people kneel,
accept Makeda, Queen of Sheba, praise
her son. My lord, this gift has made me whole . . .
I thank you, granting me my heart's desire.

A LANTERN THINLY BLOWN

Book of Esther
  Chapter 2:5,6,7
  Chapter 4:14

Esther's time in history came after the Judean people had been in captivity in Babylon for more than a hundred years.

In 539 B.C. Cyrus of Persia conquered Babylon, thus Mordecai and Esther were reared under Persian influence with Shushan, the Persian Capitol, situated on the Persian Gulf, some three hundred miles across the desert toward the west from Babylon.

Mordecai must have journeyed to Shushan with Esther, his cousin, whom he reared after her parents died, for he forbade Esther to reveal her Jewish heritage in their new locality, since the reigning king, Ahasuerus,* was Gentile. Thus when the land's most beautiful virgins were selected as candidates for the future Queen of Persia, no one knew of Esther's Hebrew background.

A Lantern Thinly Blown depicts the journey from Babylon to Shushan in Esther's remembrance. Esther seemed to feel a hero worship for Mordecai who was probably not more than fifteen years older than she, for he gained great importance in the government after Esther was chosen Queen, in approximately 510 B.C.

* Ā has ū ē rus

A LANTERN THINLY BLOWN

Esther:

I, Esther, your queen, have need to speak with you,
Asenath. When I came into this court
of women, some twelve months ago, my rue
filled heart was consoled by you, kindest of three
handmaidens given me by royal laws.
You did not envy me the attributes
of desert-lily charm that nightly draws
oasis moths which bring to me the pollen
of poppies, so to dull my love for him
who considers me a daughter, though so false.
I claim a decade's difference but a whim
of time between our births. He nurtured me
when I was orphaned, warmed me, gently refused
my naive overtures veiled in modesty.

Asenath, you are the favored one of fate,
for you are free to accept your chosen love,
while I was born a destined pawn of state,
the queen of mighty Persia. My lord, the king
is one a maid should seal in glass thinly blown,
adroit in manner, wise, though impatient; a falcon
magnificent and strong, who claims his own
in heights where sky and mountains meet in clouds.
I am blessed, chosen to calm my lord's unrest,
to hold his love. Yet outside the courtyard wall
a man sits clothed in sackcloth, waiting to test
my loyalty. His mourning torments my peace,
I must know why his lamentations do not cease.

Asenath:
Queen Esther, white dove of grace amid bevies of quail,
your handmaiden's faithfulness stems from an inner spring
of devotion. Since first I watched you tip the scale
of favor, bow with reserve toward the chancelor,
I sensed your bewilderment, saw your pride recoil
while thorns of suspicion pricked your heart. I guarded
the slaves who purified your body with oil,
selected those who fashioned your untamed ways.

In you I detected a golden substance encased
in the iridescent flame of beauty. Queen Esther,
I long have known of the man who so often paced
the street, as a tiger that stalks the length of a cage,
so this man measures the width of the palace gate,
searching the windows for one reassuring glimpse
of some loved face, perhaps to evaluate
her happiness. These hibiscus in the vase
reflect the tint that rises to your cheek;
tell me, my queen, the nature of what you seek.

Esther:
Think not that I am false to my worthy lord,
though I must know, Asenath . . . I can not rest . . .
of why my cousin Mordecai still moans
of some dark threat that echoes in stark protesting.
I can not understand, for it was he
who shrewdly exposed a plot to slay the king,
which I relayed, as a trust, to his majesty,
so why this fear of evil reckoning?

Asenath:
Queen Esther, lily among thistles, oasis of compassion
that portions life to desert creatures. Last night
when Mordecai refused your consolation,
a raiment sent as forfeit to claim his sackcloth,
I could foresee my queen might request the condition
of his welfare. Even now Hatach awaits
to ask him the reason behind his demonstration.

Queen Esther, lily among thistles, Mordecai
has confessed to palace guards he is a Jew,
that he worships the one true God. They who gratify
man's vanity fall into Satan's pit. This he said.
Thus when Haman, the king's favored spokesman, passed
    through
the street, every person knelt with eyes downcast
save Mordecai. Such defiance fostered the cue
of Haman's hatred, burning now as flame
beneath a kiln which produces molten ore
for fury's idol, the pockmarked god of vengeance.

Hatach comes! I hear the commotion through the door.
My queen, let me first receive the angry critique
that impels his voice to break with indignant pique.

Esther:
Asenath, your concern is ever my shield,
yet strength comes to him who makes his own protection.
Bid Hatach enter. Demand nothing be concealed.

Come forward, scribe. Your loyalty merits reward,
accept, with my favor, this topaz. My bondsmaid will read
the message to me in private. I wish you God's speed.

Asenath:
My queen, the winnower fastens her net of dismay
on the tree of life. The madman, Haman, decrees:
DEATH TO EVERY JEW IN PERSIA.
                                                    A survey
shall be made as the autumn moon wanes pale. The plot
strikes terror, though none would judge you one of them
with complexion tinged as a sun-kissed apricot
and hair that resembles a burnished diadem.

Esther:
The anklet of fear marks the slave. Never have I wished
to deceive my lord, though from Mordecai I learned
to hold a silent tongue, for my kinsmen have known
the dark blade of vengeance. I have often turned
to memory's terror . . . that day we left our home
in flame, driven out by soldiers seeking loot,
how we hid in a snake-infested catacomb
until our plight was discovered by Mordecai
who took us from that ravished place to the kingdom
of distant Persia. There seemed a thousand days
of desert-evil which locked us in a vacuum
of sun and thirst and endless sand. My skin
transformed to orange blisters, my hair dried white
and brittle as bone; senses blurred; my eyes paled as blue
skimmed milk. We were trapped in death's cremative light.

My parents died and Mordecai pulled me
on blanket sled by night. Now the sundial completes
the circle.
　　　　　Tell Mordecai this: Relay my plea
that our people fast and pray with me three days,
that their queen submits to the purpose in time and place.
I take an oath. To expose Haman's tyranny
and ask the king's intercession for my race.

Asenath:
Three days have embraced the earth, three nights have died,
three days of fasting, my Rose of Jericho,
cruciferous blossom that ever returns to life
with administered moisture. My queen, your flesh is gray
and withered, your body lifeless as though a knife
had pierced your breast. Come drink of this wine-nectar
from the pomelos, come taste the warmth of bread
and honey. Your God, has he given you a sign?
You must not believe that the Queen of Shushan be led
as sacrifice to save a race from death.

Queen Esther, Rose of Jericho, I rejoice
to see your lips once more touched with pomegranate pink
and to hear the vibrant cadence to your voice.
I marvel at the opalescent luster
of your skin. Yet be not deceived. Remember Vashti
whose pride cost her a throne; her fault was mild
while you force your presence upon the king, defy
the royal custom proclaimed by Ahasuerus.

129

Esther:
Asenath, you speak true wisdom, yet say no more.
Fasting has its own reward. At first
illusions sear the mind, and vultures soar
above the head of one so lost in thirst;
gaunt hunger throws the scarlet veil of Satan
across hot eyes, until the heart-flames burst
with temptation, the branding-iron of destiny.
All time drops through the hourglass; days that turn
as tumbleweed and I am whirled backward
to by beginning, to let old values burn;
resentments wither as chaff, and trivials blow
away, to reveal the larger tapestry;
each individual thread is clearly traced
through emotion's fabric. Often a mystery
is solved within the heart, as I have found.
Mordecai, I honor in filial love,
but now as woman, I have heard the sound
of troubadour winds as they caress me. I see
not the minstrel, yet fig trees sway over rippling sand
and I am held in intimate tenderness,
as does my lord, Ahasuerus, brand
his image on my senses. I can hear
the echo of his words released as song
within my pulses. Make haste with confident heart,
bring now the royal apparel. My fears are gone.
Come brush my hair, make me lovely to behold;
then shall I stand in the courtyard beneath a palm
and wait until my king ascends the throne.
Take courage, Asenath, note my inner calm.

I know not whether the depth of my lord's forgiveness
is balanced by his love, nor if his mood
be compassionate toward my request to approach his
    presence,
nor if he will choose spontaneously to preclude
my situation, extend to me his scepter.

If he fails me, angered at silence concerning my race,
then naught is left of joy. One last request,
Asenath, place a smile upon your face
for me. Now I am content. Come open the door . . .
If I perish . . . if this be destiny . . . then I perish.

Aftermath:
Queen Esther looked across the palace lawn
where swans careened upon the lake and dreamed
of months gone by, how Mordecai had saved
the King and gained his favor until it seemed
his majesty could never show his trust
enough . . . had given him the royal ring
the stamp of all authority to redeem
their people, never believing it would bring
revolt in all the provinces. How hot
the flame of hate that Haman long had fanned
and though that evil man was put to death,
ten sons had carried on, until the land
turned red beneath the swords of rioters,
til each young Haman had been captured, tried,
then executed under Mordecai,
thus peace now reigned for people far and wide,
and though she had been born for such a time
her heart was heavy with compassion born

of pity for the lost and prayed the King
might cherish her who loved, as fate, a thorn
upon the Hebrew stem of destiny,
his Rose of Sharon awaiting his Majesty.

Interlude

400 years

HOW FAR TO BETHLEHEM

St. Matthew 1:18-25
St. Matthew 2:1-12

The Star of Bethlehem has captured the imagination of men over the centuries. Excavations and ancient writings have produced astonishingly detailed information about the astronomical occurrences of the Messianic star. We now possess notes of observations concerning it from Greek, Roman, Babylonian, Egyptian and Chinese sources. People all over the world saw the star but the Magi as revealed in St. Matthew were the ones who coupled it with prophecy of the Hebrews and acted upon their convictions.

Today the modern astronomer can turn the cosmic clock at will. In his planetarium he can arrange the starry sky exactly as it was thousands of years ago, for any given year, any month, even a day.

Astronomers now have revealed that the disturbances of stars and the drawing of Jupiter and Saturn first appeared in March almost two thousand years ago, but the display was so pale that astronomers gave it little importance. Since the new star appeared in brilliance three times over a period of months, the first shadowy formation is thought by some theologians as the time of Mary's conception.

HOW FAR TO BETHLEHEM

The Christmas star has burned a brand
on eternity. Let the centuries
fall back and unfold events at that bright
millennium when prophecies
would soon congeal in time. One night
the last of May, in far off land
of Babylon, a filagree
of comets fountained from the sky,
as astronomers watched the nebulae,
watched Jupiter intensify,
then slowly move toward Pisces, drawn
it seemed, into a rendezvous
with Saturn. Then the breath of dawn
empaled the constellation, blew
out stars and left the three Magi wrapt
in ponderance. Long had Jupiter been thought
a royal star. Should they adapt
this sign to the Jewish Messiah, as taught
by prophets of old, who likewise portray
Saturn the protector of Israel?
If true, then they must be present, pay
respect to King Emmanuel.
Though now, in May, the desert heat
was more than man could bear. Perchance
the eclipse would return in October, repeat
the fusion which often took place, thus enhance
the six weeks journey to Palestine;
grant time to chart a map, to buy
provisions; camels, food, and wine,
take gifts: myrrh, gold, and frankincense.

The total would be of great expense,
the cost of such a trip would well nigh
take the total savings of the three
of them, yet not to be there, not to see
the new Messiah, so long a dream
would surely cause Jehovah to deem
them unworthy . . . so when the child
was grown, he might not be reconciled
to include Gentiles in his realm
or grant them grace beneath his helm.

And so they waited for the star,
and behold! In October it shown again,
more brilliant than before. From afar
it marked the land of the Saviour's domain.
Yes, they must start to Palestine
without delay to find the shrine.

Thus in late December, from out the night
three wisemen approached old Jerusalem.
Their star had disappeared in blight
of darkness. Now they turned to stratagem,
and asked folk beside a bubbling spring,
a merchant, a beggar, a peddler, a priest,
"Where can we find the new born king
of Jews? We have seen his star in the east."
A blankness filled and dulled each face,
bewilderment opaqued the eyes,
such prophecy they could not place . . .
"We know nothing of such a child.
Only King Herod would be so wise,
though never would he be reconciled

to such a prince." Had they been fraught
with madness, to squander a fortune, and come
so far, and in peril? Had they not dealt
with thieving Bedouin, the scum
of earth, and paid their ransom? They'd fought
through devastating sand storms, the heat
of day, the chill of night, had known
even hunger and little sleep. Defeat
like a shadow of fleshless bones was blown
across their path as they sought the gate
of Herod's Palace. Once more they asked
about the child of destiny.

The guards, confused, asked them to wait.
Soon officers appeared, who masked
their ignorance with scrutiny,
questioned the strangers from afar,
and searched with caution every beast . . .
then ushered the Magi before the king.

From his throne he smiled. "You speak of a star
that brought you this distance toward the east . . .
you seek some babe . . . you are coveting
a Messiah for the multitudes.
Come now, I have been told, and soon
my own astronomers will tell
the answer. We'll see if they are attune
with you. Magicians often intrude
on fable, believing, and often rebel
against true logic. Either *THAT*,
or my star-gazers have been remiss
of duty." Herod's words were spat

in contempt, longing to dismiss
the Magi who chose to ignore his scorn.
If Herod thought they conjured spells
of shoddy magic, he belied
his reputation. The man looked torn
by fears and doubts. The sentinels
with the head astronomer bowed in pride,
confessed that Jewish prophets wrote
of such a child that would be born
in Bethlehem. Now Herod's eyes
glowed craftily. He seemed to gloat.
"There, gentlemen, be not forlorn,
go find where your Messiah lies,
then return and tell me . . . if you find
this king . . . so I may worship him
as well." The three Magi took leave
in gratitude that they were free. How blind
if they should follow Herod's whim
for surely his plot was spun to deceive.
Still Bethlehem WAS called the place
of David. Where else could they turn their face?
Perhaps they'd rest a spell before
they traveled farther to explore . . .
then suddenly the darkened sky
began to glow. The Star again!
Its third appearance in heaven's domain.
Its burning seemed to solidify
into a new born nova fused from two
great planets, that burst into rays of blue
to the glory of the child, to ordain
him King of All. The Magi led

their camels through old Jerusalem,
through narrow streets toward the needle gate.

Now people were collecting . . . they spread
through every land, to formulate
some meaning. Was this an omen-star?

"Make way . . . how far to Bethlehem?"
the Magi cried. "Four hours away,"
an echo came. They must make haste
for Herod would now be quick to betray . . .
and they wondered how soon he would have them traced.

Out on the open road they raced . . .
the miles fell away for the star shown bright
before them. From the mountains they could hear
strange celestial music that embraced
the countryside and mingled with light
of the star that charged the atmosphere . . .
then ultimately it ceased to glide
and hung above one low hillside.
Now all their doubts were reconciled,
there the virgin was cradling the child . . .
soon now, very soon, they should draw near
their destination. How far . . . oh how far
was it still . . . to Bethlehem.

A STAR LOOKS DOWN

St. Matthew 2:2-10

A STAR LOOKS DOWN

How strange the night, thought Mary, lying deep
in fresh sweet-scented straw, the very earth
seemed mystic, all the heavens glowed with light
of shadowed purple. Joseph, keeping guard
outside the stable door, announced a star,
magnificent in size, its brilliance seemed
to hover over Bethlehem and cast
a radiance on yonder hills. A wave
of weary peace enwrapt her, pressing down
upon her being much as angel wings.
How fortunate she was to have this place,
apart from others save the animals,
God's gentle creatures, where the babe would breathe
of earthliness. There was no fear, encased
within divine embrace, she gave herself
to sleep of numb hypnotic force . . . alone
within a cone of life's creation, held
in pain's eclipse of wonder. From afar
she heard celestial music fill the air,
and then from darkness burst an infant's cry.

WINE OF BITTER HERB

St. Luke 1:5-7
St. Luke 1:39-44

Elisabeth, the mother of John the Baptist, cousin of Mary, mother of Jesus.

WINE OF BITTER HERB

Elisabeth stood watching John, her son,
depart for yonder hills on desert plain
with aching heart, thought how it had begun
some thirty years or so ago, a chain
of interlocking destinies for two
prenatal babies. She had been quite old,
her cousin Mary, very young. Both knew
that God had chosen them, and both were told
their sons would carry out His plan to save
mankind from death; that John prepared the way . . .
God's son would prove a life beyond the grave.

Today her son went forth to fast and pray,
such mystic laws were hard to understand
and harder still to follow through as planned.

Elisabeth thought back to former years
when John was small; so often he would pause
as if he heard the winds of far off spheres
that ever drew his heart to hallowed cause,
but never did she think he would withdraw
from those he loved to seek the wilderness,
to eat what he could find, to sleep on straw,
alone and waiting there in somberness.

For weeks he preached, baptizing those who wished
forgiveness of their sins, while prophecy
approached. The coming trial now wrapped in mist
would slowly lift, disclose reality.

147

Did Mary also feel the piercing pain
of giving up her son? Both, God sustain . . .

DARK TENDRILS

St. Matthew 14:1-11

Salome is not mentioned by name in scripture, but referred to as the daughter of Herodias. However, both the Bible and the dictionary list her in the lineage of Herod the Great, and Josephus also mentions her by name.

Salome, the daughter of Herod Philip I and Herodias, married Herod Philip II, the son of Herod the Great and Cleopatra.

Herod the Great married ten wives, Herodias and Cleopatra among them. *(Ch. 2:1,16,19)*

DARK TENDRILS

Salome whirled as a flame about the room
and dropped in breathless ecstasy at the feet
of Herodias who smiled and cupped her hand
beneath her daughter's chin. "Tonight, my sweet,
you will enchant the king and all his court
so he will grant you anything you ask;
what shall it be?" Salome's eyes grew bright,
"You know my heart's desire, I can not mask
my love for Philip Herod, though my pride
would keep me silent, yet *you* could persuade the king
to arrange the match. I know the family strain
is interwoven but not prohibiting,
and if you would help me, queen mother, I in turn
might request a wish desired by you. I see
by your smile there is some special thing, so speak!"

"If you should marry Philip, you too might be
condemned and made a scapegoat of judgment by one
called John the Baptist, and I would have him dead.
Tonight when the king, in generosity,
grants you a wish, then ask for the prophet's head.
Do not look aghast, such zealots receive just reward,
and for Philip, surely not so much to demand."

"My mother, I must think of the past, and fate
of other women before I obey your command.
There was the spy Delilah, the first to defy
the Hebrew's Jehovah, and from that time she failed
in health and spirit. Then there was Jezebel,
the Phoenician wife of King Ahab whose faith entailed

the worship of Baal whose altars she built in the land
of Israel. The end of the conflict found
her dead, her body left for dogs to eat.
Her daughter Athaliah, still was bound
to Baal and swearing vengeance, carried on
the encounter til Israel and Judah's ground
was steeped in blood; then when her son was slain,
she claimed the throne and issued an evil decree
to destroy the Royal Seed of Judah. But God
saved one, infant Joash, found by Jehoshebea
her mother's sister, when she searched among
the dead. For six long years she hid him inside
the temple, then brought him forth as rightful king,
while Athaliah was dragged outside on the tide
of revolt and executed. Mother Queen,
your request for the prophet's head may turn to regret."

"Salome, those women lived many centuries ago,
and stars change destiny. I am not beset
with fear. The Baptist proclaims another man
the looked-for Messiah because he has the gift
of performing miracles, but who believes
him God in flesh? The end of his reign will be swift.
Fear not, for it is I who shall take the blame."

Salome dangled a scarlet veil on her wrist
and held a purple drape up toward the light,
"My seven scarves are rainbow bits of mist,
tonight when I dance I shall drop them one by one
to intrigue the guests. I will state my wish and insist
your trophy be presented on silver tray,
in return my troth to Philip go not astray."

152

VALLEY OF VISION

St. Mark 14:3-9
St. Luke 10:38

VALLEY OF VISION

The sun had reached mid afternoon and blue
tinged shadows lengthened. Mary took a box
of Alabaster filled with ointment, sweet
with spikenard. Gracefully she draped her shawl
about it, hoping Martha would not note
or ask dull questions. Mary wanted this
to be her gift alone. The words He spoke
about his coming death had wrung her heart
and yet his own disciples had not seemed
to understand what Jesus said. They smiled
and thought this but another parable.
Now Mary walked across the room to ask
if Martha needed her, but well she knew
her sister much preferred to work alone.
As Martha checked a pitcher filled with wine
to see if it were cool, she shook her head,
she wished no help, so Mary went outside
and turned toward Simon's house where Jesus was
to be with his disciples. Mary strolled
along the narrow streets of Bethany,
past little stalls where merchants hawked their wares,
past market square where caravans had stopped
to rest and water camels, yet her mind
was not concerned with this, instead she thought
of Jesus with his mystic powers from God . . .
He looked into the souls of men, He healed
the sick and raised the dead . . . as He had brought
her brother Lazarus back to life. How strange
the Master was, for once he gave rebuke
to Martha who complained of too much work

while sitting at his feet, her hand loom set
before her nimble fingers, never still;
he claimed that Mary chose the better thing
than discipline to duty. Martha felt
he did not understand her burdened life!

As Mary neared the leper's home she felt
anxiety. How dare a woman come
here uninvited. All would think her bold
and yet she had to see Him one more time.
She had to let him know she understood
about his Kingdom far away . . . how else
could she express unuttered words except
to bring a gift. She paused before the door,
and heard the voice of Jesus from within.
A dove came winging through the trees to light
beside the fountain, cooing mournfully,
perhaps it was an omen warning her,
but nothing now could change her mind. She knocked
then pushed past servants, paused . . . and saw Him smile
at her. With eyes on Him alone she rushed
to bow before him. Quickly now she broke
the alabaster box, let free the scent
of ointment. Then confusion filled the room
for all disciples disapproved her act,
while Judas rasped that spikenard should be sold
to benefit the poor, but Mary let
the fragrance drop upon the Master's head
as dew to penetrate his hair. He spoke
a reprimand. "Let her alone. The poor
ye have always, but me you will not have
for long. The priceless ointment she has used

is for my burial . . . and for this deed
her name shall be immortal." Mary's eyes
were filled with tears as Judas left . . . alone.

THE SCARLET LILY

St. John 4:7-42

Had the woman of Samaria been a woman of the street as she is often spoken of, she could never have interested the citizens of Sychar coming outside the city to meet another man whom she had happened to meet, regardless of the prophetic powers he had revealed unto her.

The Jewish people and the Samaritan people had nothing to do with each other. The Samaritans as a race had changed through intermarriage with Assyrians who had taken them into captivity. In time, the strict commandments of Jehovah belonged to another age. This woman whom Josephus named as Nalda, might have been someone of prominence, living as she pleased according to her own standards of right and wrong.

Jesus was on his way to Galilee when he tarried by Jacob's well. When he saw the woman coming, he knew through the holy spirit that she was the link by which he could convert the fallen away Samaritans.

This woman apparently was able to contact a great number of people. Perhaps she was an entertainer, a ballad singer of events in the city amphitheater and a popular celebrity, who considered herself above reproach regardless of how she lived.

Scripture bears witness in *John 4:39* ". . . and many of the Samaritans of the city believed on him (Jesus) for the saying of the woman who testified."

Jesus seldom revealed to anyone who he was and often asked his disciples, "Whom say the people that I am?" He made an exception of the Samaritan Woman. When she admitted, "I know that Messiah cometh, which is called Christ: when he is come he will tell us all things."

Jesus said unto her, "I that speak unto thee am he." *(John 4:25,26)*

The Woman of Samaria was a "chosen one" by Jesus himself.

THE SCARLET LILY

She walked along the dusty road at noon
when Sychar women hid themselves from sun,
but she had learned how heat could melt away
the flabby weight, could purify the skin,
and ease the heart of tension. Nalda knew,
despite her years, that she was beautiful
and lithe as any girl. At times folk called
her harlot when the back was turned, but still
they came to hear her sing new ballads, pay
their gold to watch her dance. Quite frequently
girls copied styles of dress and envied her
a life of free endeavor. Few recalled
the fate of youth when her one love had gone
to war to perish; flesh to dream dust; pulse
of vibrance turned to throbbing grief and she
a widow, fourteen years of age. Some said
the young would soon forget when years lay stretched
as shadowed lanterns — habits were not formed.
They failed to understand that still her heart
compared all other men with him who once
had led her toward a spring that spilled from stone.
Ah well, those years were passed, though they had set
life's pattern, why she'd married many times,
and now preferred attention from a lord
of royal lineage, one who seemed a strange
reincarnation of the past. The sun
beat down to penetrate her tunic, fired
the copper in her bracelets worn on wrists
and ankles. Jacob's well lay there where trees
of tamarisk, and date, and sycamore,

cast soothing shade. She'd rest a bit, enjoy
those hours of solitude away from eyes
of public curiosity. She swung
her empty water jar across to rest
upon the other shoulder. She was tired,
and wondered how much longer she could dance
and never pay the bowman, striking strings
of time; when destiny would cast her out
upon the desert dunes, where loneliness
would eat away the marrow of her bones?
Such morbid thought! Within the shade a man
both young and Hebrew, rested. Odd that he
should pause within this land of enmity.
As she approached, it seemed that he might speak
to her. How strange, but certainly a fresh
experience, a new approach to shock
an audience in ballad theme. She drew
herself up proudly when he asked a cup
of water. "You request this favor, bid
of me, a woman of Samaria?"

His quick reply had changed to parable
of spirit water, which when sipped, the heart
would never thirst again. What sort of talk
was this? She laughed and asked if he were great
as Jacob, one who drilled the well so long
ago. If true, then she in turn would beg
the miracle so she would never more
be chained to water jugs, a boring task.

Her flippance was ill received. In scorn
this Jew suggested she go home and bring

her husband who could better understand.
His rudeness stirred resentment toward his kind,
of would-be holiness. She tossed her head
in unconcern. "I have no husband now."
She let her pitcher down inside the well . . .
grew tense as he began to tell of all
her marriages, that now she lived outside
the bonds of matrimony. Nalda turned . . .
His eyes, afire with prophecy now probed
her soul. She listened while the mystic spoke
in words of strange portent, that he had come
from God, so all might be enlightened here.
She backed away, confused and terrified.
Forgotten was her pitcher. Nalda whirled,
and ran toward Sychar, now astir once more
with people. Why had she been singled out
and told his mission? Could he be that man
they told about with healing power, brought
about through faith and laying on of hands?
Why had he chosen her? What had he seen
within the likes of one, a common strain
of scarlet lily, found in fields of tares,
and scattered everywhere. Was there some spark
within her heart that might light someone's path
through dark despair, that only she could reach?
Perhaps the stranger knew her gift to hold
an audience spellbound with ballad songs.
Yet it could be, this new acquaintance might
stir laughter . . . even so, the nightingale
of Sychar felt that she was destined, knew
she had to try. Tonight her songs of him
would stress the prophet's skill to tell the past

and future. People loved the mystical
and soon would seek him out to hear and judge.

A dove's call echoed over sun-scorched hills.

LETHE METHANE

All Four Gospels
St. Luke 1 - 32
Acts 1:14

LETHE METHANE

Now shock had crystallized the senses, choked
the spirit flame to vapor. Mary still
could see through tears of anguish, feel the chill
of death that soon must claim her son. John cloaked
her vision, tried to shield her. Soldiers soaked
a sponge in gall to give the Christ, their thrill
of torture jaded. Then the skull-shaped hill
was gripped in storm and guards no longer joked.

Remorseful fears outran the multitude
to wait in each man's home, accusing him
with eyes that never slept. Forked lightning split
the earth; avenging winds of doom pursued
the guilty ones to reason's farthest rim
to leave them cringing in their mental pit.

A few remained to care for Him, to place
their Lord in Joseph's sepulcher; and while
they labored Mary tried to reconcile
her heart that Christ chose death. She would erase
reality; once more she would embrace
her infant son in Bethlehem, compile
each miracle within her mind, and file
each image, keep the child in memoir's case.

Through dark they helped her walk the narrow street
toward her abode, still held in cubicle
of trance, remote, where crossroads intersect
at Then and Now, where joy and pain must meet,

but not just yet. She said, "The storm will lull . . .
then he will come." She dreamed in retrospect.

She never knew how many days had passed
nor wondered why old friends took turns to stay
with her. They came and went enwrapped in gray
obscuring fog, bewildering her. At last
a beam of sunlight pierced through clouds to cast
aside the dream that gripped her; now dismay
returned to fill her heart. She heard one say
"This sorrow pains, but we must break our fast."

It all came back in blinding agony . . .
her heart kept echoing: why was it planned
to end this way? What meaning had it made
on those who witnessed Roman Tyranny?
Their cruel deeds cut through her mind to brand
her heart, reopened wounds with grief's dull blade.

She never must forget the earnest word
that Jesus spoke, his promise to return
within three days; that each man's earth sojourn
was prelude for eternal life. She heard
again the mob, her son's death-cry which blurred
all reason, all belief, in pain's deep burn.
She then saw Magdalene in strange concern
come racing up the path . . . what had occurred?

Her mantle blowing seemed as wings set free . . .
the door burst wide and Magdalene, with eyes
tear wet, called, "Come, our Master lives! Rejoice!
Tell all the rest . . . doubt not my sanity . . .

remember how he told us he would rise . . .
now I have heard him speak with living voice!"

THE FIRST TO SEE

St. Matthew 28:25
St. Mark 16:1
St. Luke 8:2
St. Luke 16:5
St. John 19:25

THE FIRST TO SEE

To Mary Magdalene life seemed to end
beneath the cross where Jesus died in shame
between two criminals. Her thoughts now wend
through days that used to be when lust, like flame
had given her no peace, and demons spurred
her on against the will, possessed her soul
with passion, greed, and jealousy, that blurred
all reason, much as weeds that take their toll
of wheat and blossoms. So would guilt entreat
the men involved to take up stones, to call
her evil as they ran her through the street . . .
she fell . . . and waited death beneath her shawl,
then heard a stranger's voice in reprimand,
"Let one without a sin lift stone-filled hand."

No rocks were hurled and Mary lifted eyes
to see the stranger kneel to write in dust,
and soon the crowd dispersed. He spoke, "Arise,
for no man now accuseth thee, so trust
in God and sin no more." He then erased
his words and offered her his hand. His touch
held some strange magic . . . pardon He engraced
with tenderness. In shame she tried to clutch
repentance as a shield to hide behind . . .
He smiled and all the past began to fade;
she felt a certain wonder fill her mind,
felt born again, released and unafraid.
"Forgetting is the secret ministry
of God," he said, "which sets a sinner free."

Resurrection Morning
Another dawn of bits of coral, seen
as teardrops colored by reflected blood
from Jesus' side. Now Mary Magdalene,
in sorrow, wondered how the trees could bud
as usual, above a broken earth
all gashed by lightning, lanced by storm. How still
it was . . . as though the dawn awaited birth
of wind, or bird song. Mary climbed the hill . . .
perhaps she too was dead and this a dream
of being lost in mist-filled nothingness . . .
the tomb was empty, centered in a beam
of light . . . her heart seemed seared with grief's distress.

A voice spoke gently, "Mary" . . . Almost faint
she gasped, "Rabbonie" . . . knelt in awed restraint.